DK Life Stories

Helen KELLER

DK Life Stories

Helen KELLER

by Libby Romero

Illustrated by Charlotte Ager

Penguin
Random
House

Senior Editor Shannon Beatty
Senior Designer Joanne Clark

Project Editor Roohi Sehgal
Editor Radhika Haswani
Additional Editorial Kritika Gupta
Art Editor Roohi Rais
Project Art Editors Yamini Panwar, Radhika Banerjee
Jacket Coordinator Francesca Young
Jacket Designer Joanne Clark
DTP Designers Sachin Gupta, Vijay Kandwal
Picture Researcher Aditya Katyal
Illustrator Charlotte Ager
Pre-Producer Nadine King
Producer Basia Ossowska
Managing Editors Laura Gilbert, Monica Saigal
Deputy Managing Art Editor Ivy Sengupta
Managing Art Editor Diane Peyton Jones
Delhi Team Head Malavika Talukder
Creative Director Helen Senior
Publishing Director Sarah Larter

Subject Consultant Sue Pilkilton
Literacy Consultant Stephanie Laird

First American Edition, 2019
Published in the United States by DK Publishing
345 Hudson Street, New York, New York 10014
Copyright © 2019 Dorling Kindersley Limited
DK, a Division of Penguin Random House LLC
19 20 21 22 23 10 9 8 7 6 5 4 3 2 1
001–308814–Jan/19

Published in Great Britain by Dorling Kindersley Limited

A catalog record for this book is available from the Library of Congress.
ISBN: 978-1-4654-7474-2 (Paperback)
ISBN: 978-1-4654-7544-2 (Hardcover)

DK books are available at special discounts when purchased in bulk for sales promotions,
premiums, fund-raising, or educational use. For details, contact:
DK Publishing Special Markets,
345 Hudson Street, New York, New York 10014
SpecialSales@dk.com

Printed and bound in China

A WORLD OF IDEAS:
SEE ALL THERE IS TO KNOW

www.dk.com

Dear Reader,

As you read about Helen Keller's life, you realize what an amazing person she was. You can also see how easily her life could have been very different. What if her parents had put her in an institution? What if Anne Sullivan had not become her teacher? There were a lot of "ifs" in Helen's life. Fortunately for her, most of those "ifs" seemed to work out for the best.

Not everyone is so lucky. I'm sure everybody can think of someone who could use a little help. Just imagine how much better that person's life could be if someone—maybe you—stepped in. You might make a difference. You might make a friend. You might even find that helping others helps you, too. If you don't believe me, listen to Helen, who once said, "The simplest way to be happy is to do good."

Happy reading,
Libby Romero

The life of...
Helen
KelleR

Chapter 1

Into THE darkness

Helen Keller was both blind and deaf, but she wasn't always that way. As an infant, she could see and hear everything around her.

Helen was born on June 27, 1880, in Tuscumbia, Alabama, a little town in the northwestern corner of the state. The small two-room cottage where she was born was covered with vines and climbing flowers. The cottage was part of the Keller family estate. Helen's grandfather had bought the land many years earlier. Over time, the place became known as "Ivy Green," because English ivy covered the main house and the trees and fences that were around it.

Helen's father, Arthur, was a friendly man who loved to tell stories. He was very sociable, and would often invite friends to stay for long visits at Ivy Green.

Arthur came from a family with strong southern roots, and he was even related to the American South's most famous general, Robert E. Lee. Arthur had been a captain in the Confederate Army during the Civil War as well.

Robert E. Lee

WHAT WAS THE CIVIL WAR?

The American Civil War was fought from 1861-65. The Union, representing the northern states, battled against the Confederacy, which consisted of 11 southern states that wanted to form their own country. The sides disagreed about slavery, and the war was one of the bloodiest conflicts in United States' history.

DID YOU KNOW?

One of Helen's ancestors was the first teacher of the deaf in Zurich, Switzerland. He even wrote a book about how to teach deaf people.

In 1877, Arthur's first wife, Sarah, died. He now had two nearly grown sons, named William and James, to raise on his own. One year later, he married Kate Adams, Helen's mother.

Kate, a young educated woman from Memphis, Tennessee, was a true southern belle. Her father had been a brigadier general in the Confederate Army, but she was related to some of the most influential families in the North. That connection shaped many of her beliefs.

Like many southerners, Arthur lost most of his money during the Civil War. To earn a living after the war, he grew cotton and became editor of the local newspaper. To help make ends meet, Kate grew her own fruits and vegetables, raised livestock, and

---

what is a southern belle?

A young woman from the south of the United States. A southern belle often comes from a wealthy background.

also made her own butter and lard. The family's fortunes didn't improve until 1885, when President Grover Cleveland appointed Arthur as Marshal of Alabama.

One bright spot during the years of hardship was the birth of Helen, the couple's first child. In many ways, Helen took after her mother—she had the same soft golden curls and pale blue eyes, and she had also inherited Kate's intelligence.

Helen loved to imitate others, and at just six months old, she was repeating things she'd heard people say, such as "H d'ye" and "tea, tea, tea." She also said "wah-wah," for "water."

Physically, Helen was flourishing, too. On her first birthday, Helen didn't just take her first steps—she ran. Helen would later recall how she chased "the flickering shadows of leaves that danced in the sunlight." The jaunt ended quickly, though, and Helen plunked back down to the ground. Crying, she reached out for her mother's protective arms.

Then one February day, when she was just over 18 months old, Helen got sick. For several days, she slept, plagued by a high fever. The family doctor came to examine her, and he told her family that she had "acute congestion of the stomach and brain." He didn't know if Helen would live.

Then, as suddenly as it had appeared, the fever went away. Helen's family was happy and relieved—their baby, they thought, was going to be okay.

BABIES AND COMMUNICATION

No two babies are the same. But in general, babies do develop certain skills at different stages of their lives. Some of the biggest steps in learning how to communicate are:

2 MONTHS
Coos, makes gurgling sounds.
Turns head toward sounds.

4 MONTHS
Begins to babble and copy sounds.
Cries in different ways to show hunger, pain, or being tired.

But Helen's family didn't know that her eyes hurt, and that they felt hot and dry. Her family didn't notice that Helen looked toward the wall instead of following the light, which had previously intrigued her. And even as Kate tried to comfort her baby, she didn't understand why Helen seemed so scared and confused.

That all changed a few days later when Kate waved her hand in front of Helen's face and noticed that Helen didn't close her eyes. Then the dinner bell rang.

Da!

6 MONTHS
Responds to sounds by making sounds. Responds to own name.

1 YEAR
Responds to simple spoken requests. Says "mama," "dada," and exclamations like "uh-oh!"

9 MONTHS
Understands "no." Copies sounds and gestures of others.

18 MONTHS
Says several single words. Points to show someone what he wants.

It startled Kate, but Helen didn't react—and that's when Kate knew that something was wrong. Helen, her daughter who had so enjoyed the sights of beautiful flowers and the sounds of songbirds, could no longer see or hear and she'd never learned to speak more than a few words.

This was caused by her illness, which the doctor simply called "brain fever." Doctors back then didn't have the tests and tools that they have today. Looking back, however, Helen probably had either meningitis, which causes swelling of the brain, or scarlet fever.

WHAT IS SCARLET FEVER?

Scarlet fever is a disease that people sometimes get if they have strep throat. Symptoms include a bright red rash, a sore throat, and a high fever. Scarlet fever is most common in children, and it used to be a serious childhood illness. Today, doctors can treat it with antibiotics.

"The odors of fruits waft me to my southern home, to my childhood frolics in the peach orchard."

Helen Keller,
The Open Door,
1957

2

The **wild child**

The next few years were a challenge, both for Helen and everyone around her. Helen was very intelligent and also very good at getting herself into trouble!

At first, Helen relied completely on her mother for protection. When Kate sat, Helen sat in her lap, and when Kate moved, Helen clung to her skirts. As they walked around, Helen explored with her hands, and before long, she could feel her way around the house and grounds at Ivy Green.

Without the help of sight and sound, Helen relied on taste, smell, and touch to understand the world around her, and she did her best to communicate with others.

If Helen shook her head,

she meant "No," while a nod meant "Yes." Helen pushed when she wanted to say "Go," and she pulled to tell someone to "Come."

Helen used her early talent for imitation to communicate other ideas. For example, if she wanted bread, she acted like she was cutting and buttering slices of bread. If she wanted ice cream, she acted like she was making ice cream and shivered to show that she was cold.

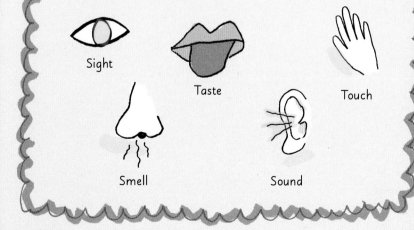

SENSING THE WORLD

There are five main senses through which animals—including people—observe the world around them. Different parts of the body can sense different things.

Sight

Taste

Touch

Smell

Sound

DID YOU KNOW?

As a young child, Helen created a vocabulary of more than 60 signs.

In this way, Helen created her own language that she used with her family and friends.

Helen's mother understood her signs, and so did Martha Washington, the young daughter of the Kellers' cook. Martha and Helen were constant playmates and, like Helen, Martha was a bit mischievous. She also knew that Helen would fight to get her way, so rather than risk getting pummeled, Martha usually gave in and did what Helen wanted.

The girls spent a lot of time in the kitchen, where they helped Martha's mother knead dough and make ice cream. They also fed the chickens that strutted up to the kitchen steps.

One day, a hen grabbed an entire tomato out of Helen's hand and ran off with it. The girls, inspired by the hen's actions, planned a heist of their own. They snatched a newly frosted cake and rushed to the woodpile to eat it!

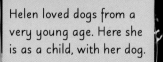

Helen loved dogs from a very young age. Here she is as a child, with her dog.

Another time, the girls were on the porch cutting out paper dolls. They soon became bored with the activity, and Helen convinced Martha to let her cut her hair. Helen snipped off a big bunch of Martha's hair with the scissors, and then Martha grabbed one of Helen's long curls and cut it off in retaliation. Luckily, Helen's mother discovered them and put an end to that game.

Helen's signs helped her to express herself, but soon they were not enough. She had started to feel people's faces as they talked because she knew other people used their mouths to communicate. However, as hard as Helen tried, she could not do this.

Helen had always been a stubborn child, but now she was frustrated, too. She would later describe the feeling of not being able to communicate as "invisible hands" holding her. The only way Helen knew how to express herself was through her actions, so she kicked and hit, and threw dishes across the room.

"I felt as if invisible hands were holding me, and I made frantic efforts to free myself."

Helen Keller,
The Story of My Life,
1903

21

Helen couldn't see or hear how she was hurting others, but her behavior only got worse. Nobody had the heart to make her stop because they felt sorry for her. Pretty soon, friends and relatives were calling Helen a monster and a wild child. They told Helen's parents that it was time to send her to live in an institution, or hospital.

The Kellers had taken Helen to several doctors over the years, and all of them said there was nothing they could do. Helen's mother refused to send her away, but then a series of events convinced her that they needed to find help.

First, there was the fire. Helen had spilled water on her apron, and to dry it, she moved

closer to the fireplace. She got too close and her clothes caught on fire. A nurse wrapped Helen in a blanket and smothered the flames before she got too badly burned.

Then, when Helen discovered how to use keys, she pulled a prank on her mother. One day, Helen locked her mom in the pantry and sat on the front porch and laughed. She could feel the floor vibrating as her mother pounded on the door. It took three hours for someone to come and rescue her mother.

The final straw came when Helen became a danger to her new baby sister, Mildred. Helen was jealous of Mildred, who now seemed to be getting all of their mother's attention. One day, Helen discovered Mildred sleeping in a toy cradle, which was one of Helen's most prized possessions. Furious, Helen toppled the cradle. Luckily, Kate caught Mildred before she fell to the floor, but the Kellers needed serious help—as soon as possible.

Finding **Anne**

Helen was now six, and she was miserable. She had tantrums every day until she was worn out. Her parents didn't know what to do to help her.

There were schools for the blind or the deaf, but none of the schools were close to the Kellers' home in Alabama. Helen was both blind *and* deaf, so finding someone willing and able to teach her seemed impossible.

Then Helen's mother read a book by Charles Dickens called *American Notes*. In that book, Dickens wrote about a woman named Laura Bridgman (1829–89).

Like Helen, Laura was both blind and deaf, but she was also educated. Laura Bridgman was the first blind and deaf person to learn language. At the age of two,

Laura got scarlet fever. When she recovered, she could no longer see, hear, or smell. She also lost most of her sense of taste.

Laura Bridgman learned language despite being blind and deaf.

Like Helen, Laura made up her own signs that she used to communicate, but her temper tantrums made her nearly impossible to manage. Just before her eighth birthday, a doctor named Samuel Gridley Howe brought Laura to the Perkins Institution for the Blind in Boston, Massachusetts. There, he taught her how to read and write.

THE PERKINS INSTITUTION FOR THE BLIND

The Perkins Institution opened in 1832. It was the first school for the blind in the United States. Perkins taught its students to explore the world with their fingertips. The school wanted its students to be educated and able to lead independent lives.

At the Perkins Institution, Laura first learned language through labels with raised letters placed on items. Later on, she learned how to fingerspell the manual alphabet in people's hands. Deaf people communicate with the manual alphabet. It uses a different hand position to show each letter of the alphabet.

Fingerspelling is a way of spelling words with hand movements into a "listener's" hand. Sometimes, people use fingerspelling if they don't know the sign for a word. They also use it to spell words for which there is no sign, like the names of people and places.

When the Kellers learned about Laura,

This is Helen with Edith Thomas, a Perkins student.

they suddenly had hope for their daughter. Helen was a smart girl—if Laura could learn to communicate, then so could Helen.

At about the same time, Helen's father heard about an eye doctor in Baltimore, Maryland. This doctor had helped some people see again after other doctors told them they would be blind forever. So in the summer of 1886, the Kellers took a train to Baltimore.

For Helen, this was a great adventure where she made friends with other passengers. One woman gave her lots of seashells to play with, and the conductor let her hang onto his coattails as he collected tickets.

When the doctor saw Helen, he said he couldn't fix her eyesight. But he did see how smart she was, and he agreed that Helen could be taught. He told the Kellers to visit Dr. Alexander Graham Bell in Washington, D.C.

Dr. Bell had taught many deaf people how to speak, so the Kellers got back on the train and went to see him. During their visit, Helen sat on Dr. Bell's knee and played with his watch. She used her signs to communicate with him, and he understood! The two became fast friends.

Dr. Bell told Helen's parents that their daughter needed a private teacher, and that they would likely find one at the Perkins Institution.

FAMOUS FRIENDS

Dr. Alexander Graham Bell (1847–1922) was a lifelong friend of Helen's. He was a scientist, inventor, and teacher of the deaf. Both his grandfather and father were speech experts, and his mother and wife were deaf. Many of Dr. Bell's inventions were machines to help the deaf. His most famous invention of all was the telephone.

That was the same school where Laura Bridgman had learned to read and write.

Helen's father wrote to the school at once, and a few weeks later, the school's director, Michael Anagnos, wrote back. He had someone who could teach Helen—her name was Anne Mansfield Sullivan.

Anne Sullivan was a recent graduate of the Perkins Institution, and she was the top student in her class. More importantly, though, she was one teacher who could truly understand what Helen was going through. This was because Anne, herself, was nearly blind.

When she was about five years old, Anne got an eye infection. Her eyes itched, so she rubbed them and the infection spread. Anne's parents had no money for a doctor, so they waited and hoped the infection would go away. It just got worse.

---

what is a graduate?

Someone who has an academic degree. A graduate will usually receive a diploma to show that they have completed schooling.

Unlike Helen, Anne had not grown up in a loving home. Anne's mother had died and her father couldn't take care of her and her younger brother, Jimmie. Her other relatives refused to help, so when Anne was 10, she and Jimmie went to live in a home called a poorhouse.

The poorhouse was called Tewksbury Almshouse, and it was a horrible, dirty place. Three months after they arrived, Jimmie died, and Anne was all alone.

Anne lived at Tewksbury for four years, and while she was there, she learned to fight for what she wanted. After she heard about Perkins—a special school for the blind—she fought for that, too. At age 14, Anne became a Perkins student.

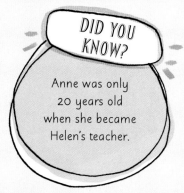

DID YOU KNOW?

Anne was only 20 years old when she became Helen's teacher.

Anne had never been to school before, and she didn't know how to read, write, add, or subtract. So she started out in kindergarten and quickly worked her way up.

However, school was only part of Anne's education. At Perkins, she also learned manners and how to control her wild temper. She learned how to speak kindly to others, and she also had two operations on her eyes so that she could see better. At Perkins, Anne got all of the tools she needed to be ready for what would become her life's work—teaching Helen.

W-A-T-E-R

It had been months since Anne had agreed to teach Helen. Anne used that time to read all of Dr. Howe's notes on teaching Laura Bridgman.

On March 3, 1887, Anne finally arrived in Tuscumbia, Alabama—Helen's hometown. Helen's mother and her stepson James went to meet her at the train station. They told Anne that they had been coming to the station for the past two days because they weren't sure when she was going to arrive.

Helen was waiting back on the front porch at their home, Ivy Green. For the past few days, she had noticed that her mother was hurrying around, and she knew someone important was coming to visit. In fact, Helen would later write that "the most important day" in her life was when her teacher, Anne Sullivan, arrived.

Helen liked visitors because they usually brought her something delicious to eat. So when Helen felt footsteps on the porch, she rushed forward to greet the visitor, and her hands flew into action. She felt Anne's face and  dress, and then she felt Anne's bag. It would not open, so Helen found the keyhole and made her sign for turning a key—she was determined to get to any treats hidden inside.

"The most important day I remember in all my life is the one on which my teacher, Anne Mansfield Sullivan, came to me."

Helen Keller,
The Story of My Life,
1903

Helen's mother told her to stop, so Helen had a temper tantrum. However, the tantrum ended quickly after Anne let Helen hold her watch. Then she and Helen went upstairs to Anne's room to begin their work together.

Anne studied Helen as the two of them unpacked her luggage. Helen was not the pale, delicate child she had expected. She was big and strong and full of energy. Anne could see that Helen was smart, but something was missing. Helen hardly ever smiled.

Helen was on a mission, and when she found a doll in Anne's trunk, she started to play with it. The doll was a gift from the blind children at the Perkins Institution. Laura Bridgman, who still lived at Perkins, had dressed it herself!

To Anne, this seemed like the perfect time to start teaching Helen. She spelled "d-o-l-l" in Helen's hand and then pointed

Anne used a doll like this one to teach Helen.

to the doll and nodded her head. Anne had noticed that Helen always nodded her head to show that something belonged to her.

It took several attempts, but soon Helen copied the motions. Helen did not understand that "d-o-l-l" spelled a word that meant "doll," but she did figure out that if she copied the motions she got to keep the doll.

For the next few days, Anne tried to teach, and Helen had a tantrum every time she failed to get her way. This behavior worked with Helen's family, but Anne needed it to stop. One day during breakfast, Anne took action.

HELEN'S DOLLS

Helen had lots of dolls when she was young. Sometimes, she treated them like they were her babies, but usually she wasn't very careful with them. She soaked one doll when she tried to feed it milk, and she planted another doll in the garden so it would grow. During one of her tantrums, she even smashed the porcelain doll Anne gave her.

Helen had bad table manners. She touched other people's plates and grabbed whatever she wanted to eat. That morning, Anne wouldn't let Helen touch her plate. Helen tried again and again. Anne refused, so Helen lay down on floor and had a tantrum. Her family was so upset by the scene that Anne asked them to leave.

Eventually, Helen stopped kicking and screaming. She stood up and walked around the table. Anne was the only other person in the room. Anne was still eating, and she wouldn't let Helen take her food. After about two hours—and fights over using a napkin and a spoon—Helen gave in and finished her own breakfast.

Anne knew that she would not be able to teach Helen until the girl learned how to obey her. She also knew that would not happen if Helen's family was around, since they gave in to her whims every time Helen had a tantrum.

So Anne talked with Helen's parents, and they agreed to let her live alone with Helen. The two of them would move into the cottage where Helen was born. Helen's family would still be nearby, but they would stay away and give Anne the space she needed to teach Helen.

Helen and Anne lived in the cottage for the next two weeks and, at first, Helen fought against everything. She even knocked out one of Anne's teeth! Soon, however, Helen seemed to understand what was happening. She and Anne were all alone, and Anne was in charge.

Helen played with her dolls, and she learned how to sew and string beads. She also learned a few new words, and she and Anne spent a lot of time exploring the gardens around the cottage.

Here's Helen a few years later in 1892, with her teacher, Anne Sullivan.

Helen would later read special books using her fingertips.

Helen's family could see them, but stayed out of their way. They were surprised at the progress Anne was making with their little girl. Helen was changing—she was quiet, and she was starting to behave for Anne.

Soon after Helen and Anne moved back into the main house, Helen could spell 21 words—but she still didn't understand that everything had a name. She didn't know that her fingers were spelling those names.

Two words that Helen kept mixing up were "m-u-g" and "m-i-l-k." She acted like she was drinking when she spelled either one. Then one day, Helen wanted to know the name for "water," and this gave Anne an idea.

She took Helen to the water pump. Anne had Helen hold her mug under the pump as cold water came pouring out. At the same time, she spelled "w-a-t-e-r" in Helen's other hand.

Suddenly, Helen understood that the wonderful, wet, cool thing flowing over her hand was "w-a-t-e-r." Helen spelled the word in her hand several times. She dropped her mug and pointed to other things for Anne to name. She learned to spell "d-i-r-t" and "p-u-m-p." She pointed to Anne and asked her name, and Anne taught her to spell the word "t-e-a-c-h-e-r." By the end of the day, Helen had learned to spell and understand 30 new words.

This is what the water pump at the Kellers' home looked like.

What is a water pump? A device that pulls up water from a well. When you push the handle of a water pump, it draws water up and out of a spout.

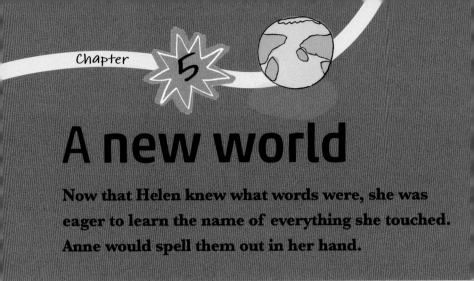

Chapter 5

A new world

Now that Helen knew what words were, she was eager to learn the name of everything she touched. Anne would spell them out in her hand.

Most children Helen's age were educated in classrooms, but Anne knew that Helen wasn't ready for that just yet. Helen couldn't learn lessons if she didn't have the vocabulary to understand them—but what was the best way to teach her the words she needed to know?

Anne found the answer after watching Helen's cousin, who was a baby. Babies, she thought, understood what words meant long before they spoke. That's because they listened to what was going on around them, and when they finally spoke, they imitated the sounds they had heard. If that's how babies learned language, Helen could do the same.

From that point on, Anne didn't just spell single words in Helen's hand, but complete sentences. She spelled out entire conversations for the young girl, with the hope that one day, Helen would know what to imitate.

Helen was behaving better now, but she was still full of energy. Anne knew that she would never get Helen to sit quietly in a classroom, but that wasn't how she wanted to teach anyway. She wanted Helen to learn through exploring her world.

UNDERSTANDING IDEAS

Early on, Helen could only learn the names of things she could touch. Then one day she was trying to make a pattern with beads, but she kept making mistakes. Anne tapped her head and spelled "t-h-i-n-k." Suddenly, Helen understood that she was thinking in her head! Some things—like thinking and love—couldn't be touched. They were ideas, but they had names, too.

The world became their classroom, and if they were indoors, they would play games. One of their favorite activities was a type of hide-and-seek, where Anne would hide specific objects, and Helen would have to find them.

Outside, they took long walks and, as they walked, Helen learned about nature and the world around her. She held crickets and felt the movement of their legs when they chirped. She held an egg just as it hatched to reveal a baby chick, and she touched new plants and discovered how they grew up from the ground.

One of their favorite walks took them to Keller's Landing. This old dock on the Tennessee River was about two miles (3.2 km) from Ivy Green. For Helen and Anne, Keller's Landing was the perfect place to play in the mud. They built dams out of rocks, dug out lakes and rivers, and formed huge mountains out of mud. Helen thought this was fun, but what she didn't realize was that it was a lesson—Anne was teaching her geography.

Anne was ready to teach Helen how to read, but first, she had to familiarize Helen with the letters of the alphabet. Anne wrote words Helen already knew in raised letters on paper cards. Then she put the words on top of the objects they named— she placed "b-o-x," for example, on top of a box.

Initially, Helen didn't understand, so Anne made the lesson simpler. She put Helen's hand on a new card. Anne spelled the shape on Helen's other hand—it was the letter A! Helen understood! By the end of the day, she knew the entire alphabet.

Next came words. Anne had a book that was written in raised letters. She placed Helen's finger on the word "c-a-t," and then she spelled "c-a-t" into Helen's other hand. Helen was thrilled because she knew the word! Soon, Helen and Anne had a new game, which involved who could find words from the book the quickest.

Once Helen understood words, Anne taught her how to sort them into sentences. Then she showed Helen how to write using a grooved writing board.

Helen loved learning, and she loved language in particular. She constantly asked questions and begged Anne to tell her stories.

Anne spelled as long and as fast as she could, but sometimes she became too tired to go on. That didn't stop Helen, though. Helen spelled in her baby sister's hand and she spelled in her dog's paw. She even carried on lively conversations with herself, spelling in her own hand!

What is a grooved writing board?

A special board placed between sheets of paper. The grooves are like lines, and they help blind writers keep their words even.

Helen never stopped, and when she became thin and pale, her parents began to worry. In order to keep Helen busy and her parents happy, Anne had Helen do less active lessons.

Helen wrote for hours, and soon her pencil writing was excellent. Anne started to teach Helen how to use braille, which is a system that allows people to read with their fingertips. With braille, Helen could write words that she could feel and read to herself.

WHAT IS BRAILLE?

Braille is a code that lets people read with their fingers. It was invented by Louis Braille, a blind French teenager, in 1825. There is a character for each letter, number, and punctuation mark. Each one is made up of a different combination of six raised dots. The dots are arranged in a cell with two columns and three rows—just like a domino.

Helen also spent a lot of time counting. First, she counted everything in the house, and then she counted all the words in her book. Helen liked counting so much that Anne joked she might even start counting the hairs on her head! Helen was eager to learn about the new and exciting world all around her!

There were many places to explore at Ivy Green, but for Helen to learn even more, she needed to explore other places as well. So when the circus came to town, the whole family went along. Helen loved the circus! She got to feed elephants and pet baby lions, and she even got to shake hands with a trained black bear! She played with monkeys and felt a giraffe's long neck. She met the circus performers, too. They let her touch their costumes and feel how they moved as they performed their routines. There was so much Helen wanted to learn!

At Christmastime, Helen went to town to celebrate at the local school. She taught several girls how to spell with their fingers and quickly made friends. For the first time in her young life, Helen understood what the Christmas holiday was, and she could share the experience with her family and friends. Helen's parents thanked Anne for making this possible. Helen was finally engaging with the world around her, and her world was about to become much bigger.

The miracle child

In May 1888, seven-year-old Helen, Anne, and Mrs. Keller took a train to Boston. They were on their way to visit the Perkins Institution.

Helen was excited about their trip. On the way, they stopped in Washington, D.C., to visit Helen's friend Alexander Graham Bell. They also went to the White House and met President Grover Cleveland.

Mr. Michael Anagnos, the director of the Perkins Institution, had invited them to visit the school, and from the moment they arrived, Helen and Anne were treated like celebrities.

Helen had written letters to the Perkins

students, and she and Anne had written to Mr. Anagnos, too. Anne had even written reports describing how she taught and what Helen had learned.

Helen and Mr. Anagnos

Mr. Anagnos was delighted with Helen's progress, and he wrote about it in the school's newsletter. However, in his excitement, Mr. Anagnos exaggerated the facts, and when the newspapers outside the school wrote about Helen, they would embellish her story even further. Helen and Anne were already famous at this point, but many of the things that were being written about them were simply not true.

---

what does embellish mean?

To add extra details that may not be true in order to make something sound better. People sometimes embellish a story.

Helen and Anne visited friends on their summer vacation in Cape Cod.

Helen didn't know the stories people told about her at Perkins, but Anne did, and she was not happy with them. She thought the truth was impressive enough.

As guests at Perkins, Anne and Helen could read the raised-print and braille books in the school's library. They could explore

the impressive collection of stuffed animals, seashells, flowers, and plants, and they could also visit nearby places like Bunker Hill and Plymouth Rock to learn about the local history.

For Helen, the best part was meeting the students she had been writing to for nearly a year. For the first time in her life, she could talk to children her age in her own language. All of the students at Perkins were blind, so they knew the manual alphabet. Like Helen, they talked with their hands.

When Perkins closed for the summer, Helen, her mother, and Anne went to visit a friend in Cape Cod, Massachusetts. While there, Helen got her first taste of the ocean—literally! Full of excitement, she ran straight into the water, but her elation, or joy, only lasted until a wave swept over her head. Then fear took over, as Helen made her way back to Anne on the beach. Shaking, she demanded to know, "Who put salt in the water?"

The next winter, Helen and Anne returned to Perkins. One of the teachers had just returned from Norway, and she told Helen about a deaf and blind Norwegian girl who had learned to speak. Helen wanted to do the same.

Sarah Fuller

Anne didn't know how to teach a blind and deaf person to speak, so she searched for the best teacher she could find. Soon, Helen began to take lessons with Sarah Fuller, the principal of the Horace Mann School for the Deaf in Boston.

As with many other things, Helen learned to speak through touch. When Miss Fuller made sounds, she put Helen's hand on her face, and she let Helen feel her lips, tongue, and throat. Helen imitated what she had felt, and in just 11 lessons, she had learned all of the basic sounds. In less than a month, Helen spoke her first sentence. She said, "It is warm."

Helen's speech was not perfect. Most people could not understand what she said, but she and Anne worked hard to make it better.

With Anne's help, Helen worked hard on her speech, but Helen was never happy with her spoken voice. Many people found it hard to understand.

The next fall, Helen wrote a story called "The Frost King." She sent it to Mr. Anagnos for his birthday, and he immediately published the story in the school newsletter. Helen's progress, after all, was good publicity for the school.

The trouble began for Helen, though, when someone wrote to the school. They said that 11-year-old Helen had copied another story called "The Frost Fairies," by Margaret T. Canby.

Helen had never heard of "The Frost Fairies," and neither had Anne, but the two stories were very much alike. After a bit of investigating, Anne discovered that someone else had read the story to Helen several years ago, and Helen had accidentally written it from memory.

Unfortunately, many people thought Helen had copied "The Frost Fairies" on purpose, including her former champion, Mr. Anagnos. At first, Mr. Anagnos said he believed Helen when she told him what had happened. Then he changed his mind and accused her of plagiarism. He also said that Anne should no longer be allowed to teach Helen.

DID YOU KNOW?

Helen and Anne loved to go tobogganing, or sledding, during Boston's snowy winters.

School leaders questioned Helen for two hours. Four of them thought she was guilty, four thought she was innocent, and, eventually, Mr. Anagnos broke the tie and voted in Helen's favor. Despite his change of heart, Helen and Anne felt betrayed.

Helen's friend, author Mark Twain, called the people who accused her of plagiarism "a collection of decayed human turnips."

What does plagiarism mean?   Using someone else's words and claiming that they are your own.

In the spring of 1893, Helen and Anne left Perkins and returned to Helen's home at Ivy Green. Helen needed some time to emotionally recover from the shame and betrayal she had experienced at Perkins.

She was upset, and for a while, she even stopped talking and reading. Helen was also afraid to write because she didn't know which thoughts were her own and which were memories of what others had said.

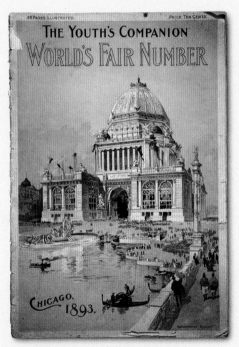

The cover of *The Youth's Companion*, World's Columbian Exposition at Chicago Issue, 1893.

After the "The Frost King" disaster, Helen struggled with her self-confidence, but then a children's magazine called *The Youth's Companion* contacted her. They asked Helen to write

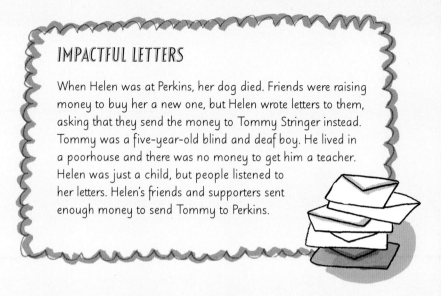

IMPACTFUL LETTERS

When Helen was at Perkins, her dog died. Friends were raising money to buy her a new one, but Helen wrote letters to them, asking that they send the money to Tommy Stringer instead. Tommy was a five-year-old blind and deaf boy. He lived in a poorhouse and there was no money to get him a teacher. Helen was just a child, but people listened to her letters. Helen's friends and supporters sent enough money to send Tommy to Perkins.

about her life. Anne thought it was a good idea, and she encouraged Helen to do it. Although Helen never wrote fiction again, she did write about her life.

Around this time, Helen also learned that her letters could make a difference in other people's lives. She slowly got her confidence back, and she began writing letters and poems to family and friends again.

Chapter 7

A star student

Now that Helen was on the mend, it was time for her and Anne to continue their pursuit of adventure and academic studies.

Dr. Bell had become one of Helen's best friends and biggest supporters. As a surprise for Anne, he and Helen planned a trip to Niagara Falls. As soon as they got there, Helen could feel the power of Niagara's water—even in their hotel, it made the glass in the windows shake! Helen was thrilled with the water's astonishing force. It was the same feeling she'd had the first time she went to the ocean.

That summer, Helen and Anne visited Chicago, Illinois. Dr. Bell had invited them to join him at the World's Fair, an exhibition that showcases the achievements of different countries. Helen was allowed to touch the exhibits, so for the next three weeks, she explored everything with her fingertips. Helen felt Viking ships and bronze statues, and she searched for diamonds. She learned about, but refused to touch, mummies. Helen also explored new inventions, such as the telephone. Dr. Bell explained how the devices worked.

Anne and Helen with friends on their trip to Niagara Falls in 1893.

After the World's Fair, Helen and Anne returned to Ivy Green, where they got back to work on Helen's education. Helen studied arithmetic, literature, French, and Latin, and she also practiced speaking. However, no matter how hard Helen tried, she knew she didn't sound like everyone else—and if there was one thing Helen wanted, that was it.

When Helen was 14,
it seemed like her dream
might actually come true.
The leaders of the Wright-
Humason School for the Deaf
in New York City said they

could help her speak like everyone else.
John Spaulding, one of Helen's wealthy
supporters, offered to pay her expenses.
So in the fall of 1894, Helen and
Anne moved to New York City. Helen
and Anne loved exploring their new city.
They walked through Central Park,
sailed on the Hudson River, and
visited the Statue of Liberty. At
her new school, Helen studied
math, geography, and French.
She learned how to speak
German and read lips.
Lip reading was a
challenge. Most deaf

Helen and Anne visited
the Statue of Liberty.

people learn how to read lips by watching other people speak, but Helen couldn't do that because she couldn't see. So Helen learned by touch, just like she did when she first learned to speak. Helen struggled when people spoke quickly, but she soon learned how to read lips.

Helen also worked hard to make her voice easier to understand, but she wasn't as successful with this endeavor. The goal was to improve her voice—not just how she said words, but the way her voice sounded. She even took singing lessons, but they didn't work. No matter how hard Helen tried, it was still hard for other people to understand what she said.

During Helen's second year at the Wright-Humason School, both her father and Mr. Spaulding died. Helen had recently become very religious and took comfort in her beliefs. She also kept busy preparing for her next goal—Helen wanted to go to college.

Helen, however, wasn't ready for college yet because she still had a lot to learn. She couldn't get what she needed at the Wright-Humason School, so it was time to go somewhere else.

Anne found the perfect place—the Cambridge School for Young Ladies. Many girls went there to prepare for Radcliffe College, but none of those girls were blind and deaf.

Helen had to get special permission to attend, and she also needed money to cover the costs. Luckily, her friends came to the rescue, and created a fund to pay her expenses. Learning at the Cambridge School was challenging. None of the teachers could fingerspell, and the school didn't have any books written in raised print or braille.

It was up to Anne to relay everything to Helen. Helen had to remember it all and type it up later.

Eventually, Helen's supporters sent a few braille books, and Arthur Gilman, the school's principal, learned how to fingerspell. Helen's German teacher learned to fingerspell, too. Best of all, Helen's mother and little sister, Mildred, came to visit at Christmas. Mr. Gilman even invited Mildred to stay and study at the school.

HELEN'S COLLEGE DREAM

College was not a new dream for Helen. As a young girl she announced that she wanted to go to Harvard, but that was impossible. At the time, Harvard was only a college for men. So Helen set her sights on Radcliffe College, which was Harvard's partner school for female students.

The year flew by and Helen
passed all of her classes, two
of them with honors.

Since Helen's first
year had been such a success,
Mr. Gilman decided she
would be ready for Radcliffe
in just three more years. Helen's
second year at Cambridge, however,
did not go as well as her first.

Arthur Gilman

Unfortunately for Helen, Mr. Gilman wanted
her to study more math. Helen hated the subject.
Now she would have to take even more advanced
math classes and, to pass, she would need
the help of an excellent tutor.

To complicate matters, many
of the supplies Helen had
ordered hadn't arrived. One
of those items was a new
braillewriter—a sort of typewriter
that printed raised letters in
braille. Helen needed this
for her classes.

In addition, Helen's classes were bigger than ever before. Her teachers no longer had time to give her special instruction, so everything fell to Anne. Anne's eyesight was getting worse, and, for the first time, Helen worried that Anne wouldn't be able to keep up.

Just as things started to get better, Helen got sick. Mr. Gilman blamed Anne, and he wrote to Helen's mother and said Anne was pushing Helen too hard. He said she should fire Anne and put him in charge of Helen's education. Mrs. Keller was worried about her daughter, so she agreed.

Helen and Mildred were
devastated when Anne left.
So was Anne, but she wasn't
about to give up. That night,
Anne sent telegrams to Mrs.
Keller, Dr. Bell, and Joseph E.
Chamberlin, who was the
editor of *The Youth's Companion*.

The next day, Anne returned to the
school. Then Mr. Chamberlin arrived, and he
invited Anne and the Keller girls to stay with
him. When Mrs. Keller arrived at Cambridge
and saw how unhappy her daughters were, she
removed the girls from the school. After that,
Helen and Anne stayed with the Chamberlins.

Once there, Helen worked one-on-one with
her tutors, and she learned quickly.
At the end of June 1899, Helen
was finally ready to take her
college entrance exams.
Radcliffe, however, wouldn't
let Anne spell the questions
in Helen's hand. The college

DID YOU
KNOW?

Helen could read five
languages in braille—
English, French, German,
Greek, and Latin.

wanted to make sure that Helen was doing the work herself, so the exams were copied into braille so that Helen could read them herself.

There were three different dot reading systems at the time, and Helen knew all of them. For math, however, each one used different signs and symbols. Helen was unfamiliar with the symbols they used on the test, and had only two days to learn them!

Because of this, the tests were harder for Helen than they should have been, but Helen passed them anyway. Her dream had come true—Helen was going to go to college.

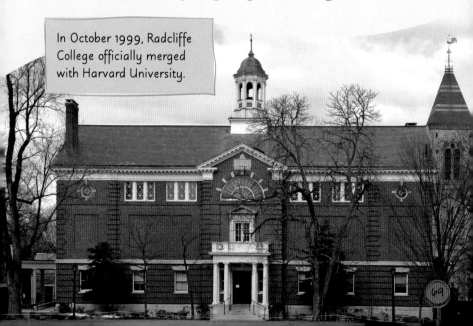

In October 1999, Radcliffe College officially merged with Harvard University.

Chapter 8

Author AND graduate

Helen had tackled many obstacles, but now she faced another challenge. The dean of Radcliffe wanted her to wait a year before starting classes.

Helen did not want to wait another year. She had even been accepted to two other prestigious, or well-respected, colleges—Cornell University and the University of Chicago. She turned them both down, however, because even though she had other options, she wanted to go to Radcliffe. So Helen agreed to the dean's demands.

For the next year, Helen studied with a private tutor. Then, Radcliffe finally agreed to let her start taking classes, but there was one condition—Helen had to take her tests alone.

What is a dean?

Head of a college or university. A dean can also be the head of a college department.

This was due to a misconception, or false belief, that Anne might have been the true genius in their partnership. Because of this, Anne could fingerspell for Helen in class, but she could not be there when Helen took tests.

Instead, Helen would have to take her tests in a room all alone, where a teacher would type the tests in braille, and Helen would answer in braille. The head of the college would be there to supervise.

At the time, many people didn't believe that a blind and deaf girl like Helen could succeed in school, and others thought she shouldn't go to college because she was a woman. Back then, many people thought women were fragile, and that their minds and bodies would be damaged by higher education. Fortunately, we know better than that today.

Helen had dreamed about going to Radcliffe for years, but college was not what she had expected. Helen thought that the professors would share greatness and wisdom, but they simply taught lessons. What's more is that they taught so quickly that Helen had trouble keeping up, and there was so much work that Helen had no time left to just sit and think. To make matters worse, all of the reading made Anne's eyesight weaker than ever.

College was lonely for Helen, too. She was different and she was also famous, so she didn't fit in. The other girls tried to be nice—they even got her a dog. However, without Anne's help, Helen could only communicate directly with two students. One girl knew how to fingerspell, and another had learned braille, but because she could communicate with so few fellow students, it was hard for Helen to make friends.

DID YOU KNOW?

Helen loved dogs. In 1938, she owned the first Akita in the US.

The students at Radcliffe gave Helen a dog, which she named Phiz.

It wasn't much better with the teachers. Only one professor learned how to fingerspell, but most of the other teachers and school leaders ignored Helen and Anne.

One professor who didn't ignore Helen was Charles Copeland. Helen took Professor Copeland's English class in her sophomore year at Radcliffe. She thought his lectures were interesting and witty, and he thought her writing was excellent. Professor Copeland even said that Helen was one of the best students he had ever had.

Charles Copeland

One day, Professor Copeland told the editor of the *Ladies' Home Journal* about Helen's writing. The editor then offered Helen $3,000 to write six articles about her life.

---

what is a sophomore? A second-year college student. Sophomore can also mean the second year of college.

Helen and Anne were already busy with classes, but that was too much money to turn down, so Helen agreed to write the articles.

Ladies Home Journal.
Cover of the American magazine for July 1902.

However, it didn't take long for Helen to realize that she needed help. Adding monthly deadlines to her classwork was too much for her to handle alone. Helen needed someone to edit her work, and she found the perfect person in John Macy. He helped Helen turn her essays from Professor Copeland's class into articles and, later, a book.

John Macy was an English instructor at Harvard University, and he had the time, intelligence, and skills to help Helen craft her articles. He even learned how to fingerspell so he could talk with Helen directly himself.

Helen in her cap and gown, which is what people wear on their graduation day.

With John's help, Helen finished her articles, and when he suggested that she expand the articles into a book, she agreed. He even found her a publisher.

DID YOU KNOW?

The $3,000 Helen was paid for her articles was equal to almost $85,000 in today's money!

Helen's book, called *The Story of My Life*, was published in 1903 during Helen's junior, or third, year at Radcliffe. Sales for *The Story of My Life* started out slowly, but it became an international bestseller.

One year later, Helen graduated from Radcliffe. It was also her 24th birthday, and with Anne by her side, she proudly accepted her diploma. She had earned a bachelor of arts degree and graduated from college with honors.

Helen's opinions

Helen had her diploma, but now she faced the same question all other new college graduates must answer: *What do I do next?*

For Helen, that question was complicated. She was blind and deaf, and she was also a woman. Because of prejudiced attitudes toward people like Helen, her job options were limited.

Helen's supporters had paid most of her expenses up until now, but she wanted to make her own money so she could support herself. Since *The Story of My Life* had become an international bestseller, Helen and Anne were more famous than ever.

After her first book's success, Helen decided to become a professional author. Not only would that help pay the bills, it would also keep her in the spotlight. That was important because Helen really wanted to make a difference. She wanted to help other blind and deaf people, just as people had helped her.

Helping other people was nothing new for Helen. As a child, she had written letters asking her supporters to send money to educate other blind and deaf children. While at Radcliffe, she had spoken to legislators in New York and Massachusetts, asking them to fund more job training programs for blind people.

Helen had also written an article called "I Must Speak" for the *Ladies' Home Journal.* In the article, she told readers about an eye infection that mothers can pass on to their babies. The cure was simple—babies just needed special eye drops.

The eye drops didn't cost much, but not all parents could afford them. Tragically, babies who had this infection and didn't get the eye drops would lose their eyesight.

Helen had always believed there was no way to prevent blindness, but now she knew that this was not the case. Knowing that so much blindness could have been prevented made her angry.

Helen saw the connection between blindness and poverty. She wanted to learn more about the struggles poor people faced, so she visited their neighborhoods. She talked with workers and immigrants to learn about their lives. She wanted to know how she could help because Helen felt it was important to improve the lives of others.

HELEN AND THE ACLU

Helen didn't just talk and write about the causes she believed in—she took action. In 1920, Helen and nine other people founded the American Civil Liberties Union (ACLU), an organization devoted to protecting the freedoms and rights of all workers. The organization is still active today with more than 500,000 members in all 50 states.

"We are never really **happy** until we try to **brighten** the lives of others."

Helen Keller, undated

Throughout her life, Helen had learned from many different people, and one person who had made a big impact on her beliefs at this time was John Macy. Helen had come to admire John when he edited her book. In addition, Anne had fallen in love with him, and when John and Anne got married in 1905, Helen lived with them.

Helen

Helen with John and Anne, 1900.

Like many Americans at the time, John was a socialist, which means he didn't think that rich business owners should control all of the country's wealth. He thought that everyone should have an equal share.

John and his friends would often get together, share popcorn and cider, and talk about their political beliefs. Helen and Anne joined them as well. Helen loved the lively discussions and she agreed with what they said. John gave Helen many books to read so she could learn more about socialism, and in 1909, Helen joined the Socialist Party, too.

This was a good time for the three friends. With John's help, Helen published two more books. Anne and John were happily married, and Helen loved living with them. John often took Helen for rides on a bike built for two people—Helen loved it when they went really fast!

Best of all, Helen and Anne's relationship was changing. Instead of simply being teacher and student, Helen and Anne were becoming friends.

DID YOU KNOW?

The FBI was suspicious of Helen because she wrote about socialist subjects.

But there was one problem—money. Helen was working, but she wasn't earning enough money to support herself and pay Anne's salary. She still needed the help of her wealthy friends, and that, unfortunately, went against her socialist beliefs.

As a socialist, Helen wanted to help workers, for whom she believed in equality, fair wages, and good working conditions. She felt especially bad for women and children, since they often had the worst jobs and had little or no power to change anything.

Many of Helen's supporters were capitalists who owned the businesses where these people worked. So in the beginning, Helen kept quiet about her beliefs, but she and Anne were running out of money.

Andrew Carnegie was one of the wealthiest people in the world. He had sold his business and wanted to share his wealth with others. In 1910, he offered to give Helen an annual allowance, and although Helen needed the money, she kindly refused.

Andrew Carnegie

Instead, Helen wrote another book called *Out of the Dark,* in which she wrote

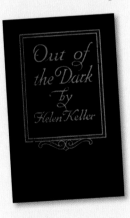

about her socialist beliefs. The book did not sell a lot of copies. People didn't care about Helen's politics—they wanted to know more about her life.

Things were not going well for Helen and Anne. Anne and John's marriage was falling apart, and John had left. Helen had given up hope of supporting herself as an author, and money was tighter than ever. The solution, she convinced Anne, was to go on a lecture tour together.

Their first lecture took place in February 1913, but what they hadn't counted on was Helen's stage fright. When it was Helen's turn to speak onstage, she froze, and only managed to whisper. When Helen was finally done, she ran from the stage and burst into tears.

Even though it was difficult, Helen worked on her stage fright, and the two women continued on their tour. A few months later, however, Anne got sick and because they were stuck in a hotel, there was nothing Helen could do to help her. When Anne recovered, they went home.

Helen felt helpless to change her financial situation, so she wrote a letter to Andrew Carnegie. The two had become good friends over the past three years. She asked if his offer of an allowance was still good—luckily for her, it was. Despite her socialist beliefs, this time Helen accepted.

Anne and Helen during their lecture tour of the Northeastern United States in 1913.

Anne and Helen in New York at the International Flower Show in 1913.

10

Finding her voice

For the next several years, Helen and Anne traveled almost constantly. They went around the country giving their lectures.

They didn't go on their lecture tour alone this time. Helen's mother often went with them, and if she didn't, Polly Thomson went along instead. Polly was a Scottish

immigrant that they had hired to help Anne with all of her duties. Anne was struggling with her workload, and she was also very sad because she and John had now separated permanently.

Helen felt strange being in the spotlight, but she had a lot

Polly Thomson

to talk about. In addition to being a socialist, she was now a suffragist as well. This means that she supported women's rights. Helen was also a pacifist, which means she was against war.

The United States was getting ready to enter World War I (1914–18). Helen thought this conflict was just a way for capitalists to make more money, so she encouraged working class people to fight against the war.

Helen's lectures were a huge success, and she sometimes spoke before crowds of more than 2,000 cheering people. However, in the summer of 1916, they came to a halt. Anne was sick and went away to recover, and Polly was in Scotland visiting her family. Helen went to stay with her mother in Alabama, and while she was there, she fell in love.

Helen, who was now 36 years old, never thought she would marry, but Peter Fagan swept her off her feet. Peter, age 29, was a socialist and a newspaperman. Helen had hired him as a temporary secretary.

The couple planned a secret wedding—they even took out a marriage license. However, their plans were ruined after Helen's mother read about the marriage license in the newspaper.

Helen's entire family was against the marriage, and so was Anne. None of them thought Helen should marry and have children. They made Peter leave, and the pair never met again.

Sadly, this was not the only part of her life that was falling apart. The US had entered World War I, and Helen's socialist and pacifist ideas were no longer popular. Some people even thought her ideas were dangerous and, because of this, fewer people wanted to hear Helen speak.

WHY COULDN'T HELEN GET MARRIED?

In the early 1900s, it was against the law in many parts of the United States for women with disabilities to get married and have children. Helen's family and friends didn't think she should get married, even though they knew this made Helen unhappy. Today, laws like this are illegal because they discriminate against people with disabilities.

Anne returned home after she recovered from her illness, and after going over their finances, she had bad news—they could no longer afford to keep their home. Helen, Anne, and Polly would have to move, and they also needed a new source of income. Fortunately, Helen's luck was about to change.

In early 1918, a Hollywood producer contacted Helen because he wanted to make a movie about her life. He promised to pay Helen $10,000 when filming began, and he said that she could earn up to $100,000 if the film was a success. The offer seemed too good to pass up.

Helen was excited about this new idea. A movie would allow her to communicate with more people than ever before. More importantly, though, it would give her the money she needed to take care of Anne.

The movie, called *Deliverance*, almost didn't get made. Just before filming began, Helen gave a speech supporting a union and its radical ideas. The film's producer panicked—he was afraid that the government would harass them if Helen kept giving speeches like that. In addition, he was worried that theaters would refuse to show their film. Helen agreed to stop giving speeches, and then she, Anne, and Polly went to Hollywood to make the movie.

Helen enjoyed making the film, but she wasn't entirely happy with the final product. She wanted the movie to be factual, but the producer wanted to create suspense. Critics gave the movie good reviews, but few people went to see it. Beyond the initial $10,000 she got when filming began, Helen didn't receive any more money for making

While in Hollywood, Polly, Helen, and Anne met many famous stars. Charlie Chaplin, standing, even invited them out to dinner.

the movie. However, Helen's career in entertainment was far from over.

Bitten by the acting bug, Helen decided to tell her story in a new way. She created a vaudeville act based on the lectures she and Anne had given years earlier. At the time, vaudeville was even more popular than films. Its acts included singers, dancers, animals, and

what is vaudeville? A type of theater show popular in the US in the 1920s.

acrobats. Helen's friends tried to talk her out of her idea, but she insisted—she and Anne needed the money.

Helen and Anne's act premiered on February 24, 1920, at the Palace Theatre in New York City. They were paid $2,000 a week, and at the time, they were some of the highest-paid vaudeville performers in the world.

Helen loved the excitement of the live act, but Anne did not. Anne hated rushing around. She hated the noise, and the stage lights hurt her eyes. Plus, she kept getting sick, but she stuck with it for the money.

In November 1921, Helen and Anne were about to give a performance in Los Angeles, California. Helen received word that her mother had passed away, so she and Anne went home. When they arrived, Helen learned that her dear friend Alexander Graham Bell had died, too.

Helen and Anne were exhausted, and Anne's health was worse than ever. These challenges proved to be too much, and they never returned to vaudeville.

Helen and Anne in costume for one of their famous vaudeville performances.

Chapter 11

Helping THE blind

A new opportunity came in 1924. Helen and Anne were asked to become fundraisers for the American Foundation for the Blind (AFB).

The AFB was quite a new organization, but it had already developed a single braille code for the nation. It had created a braille printing press so more books for the blind could be published, and its members also helped blind people find jobs.

Teaming up with the AFB was good for everyone. Helen could focus on a cause that was dear to her heart—helping the blind—and she and Anne would receive a regular income. The AFB, in turn, would get two powerful names to bring attention to its cause.

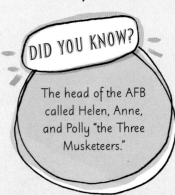

DID YOU KNOW?

The head of the AFB called Helen, Anne, and Polly "the Three Musketeers."

It quickly became clear just how much influence Helen's name had. She and Anne raised $21,000 at their very first fundraiser. After talking with President Calvin Coolidge, he agreed to serve as the AFB's honorary chairman.

President Calvin Coolidge

Helen held fundraisers in her home, and she spoke in churches and town halls. She and Anne worked hard to teach people about blindness, but after three years, it was time to take a break.

Helen's influential name attracted wealthy donors like Henry Ford, who gave money to the AFB.

Helen wanted to write more books, so she hired an editor named Nella Braddy Henney to help her. The first book, *My Religion*, was published in 1927. The second, *Midstream: My Later Life*, came out in 1929, but it wasn't as popular as Helen had hoped. People wanted to read about her childhood—they didn't care as much about Helen's life as an adult.

That, however, was the least of Helen's worries. Anne's eyesight was worse than ever, and in 1929, she had to have surgery to remove

The US Capitol Building, which is the home of Congress.

her right eye. So when Helen went to Washington, D.C., to speak to Congress, Polly went with her instead.

The trip was a success, and Congress agreed to give $75,000 for the printing of more braille books. This was the first time the US government had ever supported a program for the blind.

Nella Braddy Henney and Helen in Garden City, New York, 1940.

DID YOU KNOW?

Helen was an excellent typist. She typed better than Anne or Polly.

In April 1931, Helen, Anne, and Polly went to New York. They represented the AFB at its first international conference of workers for the blind. Helen spoke before people from 32 different countries. After this, Helen would go on to make many international trips as an AFB ambassador.

Not all of Helen's international travel was for work, though. When they needed a break, she, Anne, and Polly went to Scotland to visit with Polly's family. In 1932, during the second of three visits, they learned that John Macy had died. He and Anne had been separated for years, but Anne was still very upset. She even paid for his funeral.

Helen's influence at home was growing. She became friends with President Franklin Delano Roosevelt (FDR), and she encouraged him and other lawmakers to help the blind.

---

what is an ambassador?

Someone who is a representative, often abroad, of an organization, country, or group of people. Helen was an ambassador for the AFB.

President Franklin D. Roosevelt signing the Social Security Act
at the White House in Washington, D.C., August 14, 1935.

In 1935, FDR signed the Social Security Act,
which gave unemployment insurance, retirement
funds, and assistance to children and the
disabled—including the blind.

One year later, Helen suffered her greatest
loss of all. Anne fell into a coma, and on
October 20, 1936, she died. Devastated by the
loss of their friend, Helen and Polly went back
to Scotland to recover.

Chapter 12

Honoring Helen Keller

Helen continued to spread her message after Anne was gone. She worked hard to make a difference in other people's lives.

In April 1937, Helen and Polly sailed to Japan. Helen carried a goodwill message from President Roosevelt to the Japanese people. In Japan, Helen gave 97 speeches in 39 cities, and huge crowds came to hear her speak. After her tour, there was a national call to help people with disabilities in Japan.

Helen and Polly continued their tour in Korea and Manchuria. Fearing the outbreak of war, the president of the AFB tried to convince them to come home, but Helen was still mourning Anne. Touring was Helen's way of handling her grief, so she continued to travel.

Then Japan invaded China. For the next month, Helen and Polly traveled in darkened trains, and Helen gave speeches in dimly lit auditoriums. This was because dark buildings were less likely to be targeted by bombs.

Travel abroad was becoming too dangerous, so the rest of the tour was canceled, and Helen and Polly returned home. Helen published another book, *Helen Keller's Journal*. Then she and Polly moved to Westport, Connecticut. They named their home Arcan Ridge after one of their favorite places in Scotland.

Helen

Polly and Helen during their tour of Japan.

In 1939, World War II (1939–45) began when Germany invaded Poland. When Japan bombed Pearl Harbor in Hawaii on December 7, 1941, the US entered the war on the side of the Allies (Great Britain and the Soviet Union). Helen had disapproved of World War I, but she agreed that the US had no choice but to fight now.

Helen wanted to help the soldiers, so the AFB arranged for her and Polly to visit military hospitals. Many soldiers had serious injuries that meant they would be disabled for the rest of their lives. Helen was a good role model for these soldiers because she gave them hope. Like her,

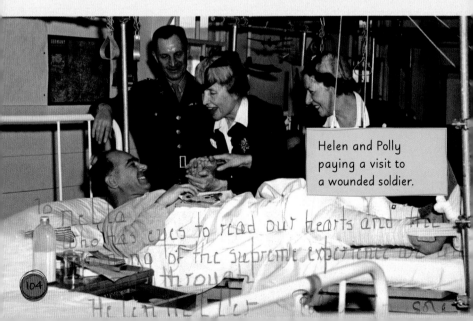

Helen and Polly paying a visit to a wounded soldier.

WORLD WAR II

During World War II, the Axis countries (Germany, Italy, and Japan) fought the Allies. The war ended after the US dropped atomic bombs on the Japanese cities of Hiroshima and Nagasaki. After the war, Helen was America's First Goodwill Ambassador to Japan in 1948.

they could become something — it didn't matter that they were disabled.

After the war, Helen and Polly went back on tour. Between 1939 and 1957, Helen spoke before people in 39 countries on five continents and encouraged people to help make the lives of blind and deaf people better.

While on tour in Rome, Helen received word that her home in Connecticut, Arcan Ridge, had burned down. She and Polly lost everything, including 20 years of notes Helen had collected for a book she was planning to write about Anne. Helen's friends built her a new home, Arcan Ridge 2, and it was almost identical to the house it had replaced.

Alabama State Quarter, issued in 2003.

Helen's work wasn't going unnoticed. In 1953, she was nominated for a Nobel Peace Prize. She didn't get that, but over the next several years, she did receive enough awards to fill an entire room. Among them was the Presidential Medal of Freedom, which President Lyndon B. Johnson awarded her in 1964. (Years later, the US Treasury would honor Helen by putting her image on the Alabama State Quarter, which also features her name in braille.)

Once again, Helen's story was captured on film. Nancy Hamilton, who was a friend of Helen's, produced a documentary about Helen's life. *The Unconquered*, which was later renamed *Helen Keller in Her Story*, was released in 1954.

Helen winning an Academy Award®, 1955.

In 1955, it won an Academy Award® for the best feature-length documentary film.

The Miracle Worker, a play about Helen's childhood, opened on Broadway in 1959. The play won the 1960 Pulitzer Prize, and it was later made into a movie. The actors who played Helen and Anne both won Academy Awards®.

In the midst of all this activity, Helen and Polly continued to travel. In 1955, they went to Asia. Over five months, they covered 40,000 miles (64,000 km). In 1956, they visited Polly's family in Scotland. In the spring of 1957, they went on their last trip as AFB ambassadors and, sadly, in March 1960, Polly died.

In October 1961, Helen suffered a stroke, which occurs when the brain's blood supply is blocked. Over the next few years, Helen had more strokes, and then she developed diabetes. It was hard for Helen to travel or even walk. She could no longer make public appearances, but she spent time with her friends at home.

In late May 1968, Helen had a heart attack. A few days later, she died peacefully in her sleep. It was June 1, 1968, and Helen was 87 years old. She had accomplished so much during her lifetime that every year since her death, people go to pay their respects to her in her final resting place at the National Cathedral in Washington, D.C. There, she is buried next to her lifelong companions and friends, Anne and Polly.

Helen, who had never feared death, was gone, but her life, like her message, will never be forgotten. In 1977, a war relief fund that Helen helped found during World War II was renamed Helen Keller International (HKI) in her honor. Today, HKI has more than 180 programs to help improve the lives of blind and poor people in 22 countries, and it presents several awards in Helen's name.

One of the most important activists of the 20th century, Helen Keller was and always will be remembered as an inspirational symbol of strength.

Helen's
family tree

Grandfather

David Keller
1788–1837

Mary Moore
1796–1875

Grandmother

Father

Captain Arthur H. Keller
1836–1896

Half brother

James Keller
1867–1906

Half brother

William Simpson Keller
1874–1925

Grandfather

General Charles Adams
1817–1878

Grandmother

Lucy Everett
1828–1889

Mother

Kate Adams
1856–1921

Helen Keller
1880–1968

Sister

Mildred Keller
1886–1969

Phillips B. Keller
1891–1971

Brother

Helen was Arthur and Kate's first child together

Mildred married Laban W. Tyson and had three daughters.

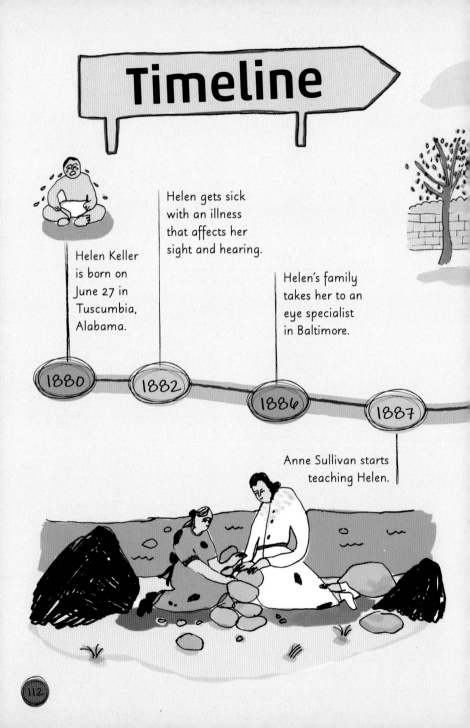

Timeline

Helen gets sick with an illness that affects her sight and hearing.

Helen Keller is born on June 27 in Tuscumbia, Alabama.

Helen's family takes her to an eye specialist in Baltimore.

1880

1882

1886

1887

Anne Sullivan starts teaching Helen.

Helen starts studying at Radcliffe College.

Helen starts attending the Perkins Institution for the Blind.

1888   1891   1894   1896   1900

Helen begins her studies at the Cambridge School for Young Ladies.

Helen is accused of plagiarizing her short story, "The Frost King."

Helen and Anne move to New York City. In the same year, Helen enrolls at the Wright-Humason School for the Deaf.

Helen graduates from Radcliffe College. She becomes the first deaf and blind person to graduate from college.

Polly Thomson joins Helen's household.

Helen stars in a silent film, *Deliverance*, which is based on her life. In the same year, she starts her career as a vaudeville performer.

1903 1904 1914 1915 1919

Helen's autobiography, *The Story of My Life*, is published.

Helen co-founds her first charity, a war relief fund for Allied soldiers.

Helen's beloved companion and teacher, Anne, slips into a coma and passes away on October 20.

Helen wins an Oscar® for *Helen Keller in Her Story*, a documentary film about her life.

Helen dies on June 1, just before her 88th birthday.

Helen becomes a spokesperson for the American Foundation for the Blind (AFB).

1920 1924 1936 1955 1964 1968

Helen co-founds the American Civil Liberties Union (ACLU) with nine other people.

Helen receives the prestigious Presidential Medal of Freedom.

Quiz

 1   What was the name of Helen's childhood home in Alabama?

 2   What was Helen's younger sister's name?

 3   Who taught Helen how to read and write?

 4   What is the system that lets people read with their fingertips?

 5   Who gave Helen her first speech lessons?

 6   Which college did Helen attend?

 7   Who helped Helen craft her *Ladies' Home Journal* articles into her first book?

Do you remember what you've read?
How many of these questions about
Helen's life can you answer?

 What is the name of Helen's first, and most famous, book?

 What was the first movie made about Helen's life called?

 For which charitable organization was Helen an ambassador?

 What do you call someone like Helen who supports women's rights?

 What was the war relief fund that Helen helped to found during World War II renamed in 1977?

 Answers on page 128

Who's who?

Anagnos, Michael
(1837–1906) educator and director of the Perkins Institution for the Blind

Bell, Alexander Graham
(1847–1922) scientist, friend of Helen's, and inventor who is best known for designing the first working telephone

Bridgman, Laura
(1829–1889) first blind and deaf person to learn to read and write

Carnegie, Andrew
(1835–1919) philanthropist, friend of Helen's, and one of the wealthiest businessmen of the 19th century

Chamberlin, Joseph E.
(1851–1935) editor of *The Youth's Companion* and friend of Helen's

Cleveland, Grover
(1837–1908) President of the United States from 1885 to 1889 and 1893 to 1897

Copeland, Charles
(1860–1952) Helen's professor at Radcliffe

Fagan, Peter
(birth and death dates unknown) newspaperman, Helen's temporary secretary, and the man she almost married

Fuller, Sarah
(1836–1927) principal at the Horace Mann School for the Deaf who gave Helen her first speech lessons

Gilman, Arthur
(1837–1909) educator, principal of Cambridge School for Young Ladies, and co-founder of Radcliffe College

Howe, Samuel Gridley
(1801–1876) founder of Perkins Institution for the Blind, and Laura Bridgman's teacher

Keller, Arthur
(1836–1896) Helen's father

Keller, James
(1867–1906) Helen's half brother

Keller, Kate
(1856–1921) Helen's mother

Keller, Mildred
(1886–1969) Helen's sister

Keller, Phillips Brooks
(1891–1971) Helen's brother

Keller, William Simpson
(1874–1925) Helen's half brother

Lee, Robert E.
(1807–1870) Commander of the Confederate Army during the Civil War, and one of Helen's relatives

Macy, John
(1877–1932) writer, editor, and husband of Helen's teacher, Anne

Roosevelt, Franklin D.
(1882–1945) President of the United States from 1933 to 1945

Spaulding, John
(1832–1896) one of Helen's wealthy supporters

Sullivan, Anne
(1866–1936) Helen's teacher, friend, and lifelong companion

Twain, Mark
(1835–1910) pen name of American writer Samuel L. Clemens, and friend of Helen's

Thomson, Polly
(1885–1960) Helen's companion and helper

119

Glossary

ambassador
someone who is
a representative,
often abroad, of an
organization, country,
or group of people

antibiotic
drug used to treat
bacterial infections

atomic bomb
powerful bomb that
releases nuclear energy
when it explodes

auditorium
large building used
for speeches or
performances

braille
system of raised
dots for blind people
to read using their
sense of touch

braillewriter
sort of typewriter
that prints raised
letters in braille

capitalist
person who invests
his or her money
in privately owned
businesses for profit

congestion
medical condition in
which there is a blockage
in part of the body

Congress
law-making branch
of the US government

dean
head of a college or
a college department

diabetes
a disease that results from too much sugar in the blood

embellish
to add extra details that may not be true to make something sound more interesting

FBI
Federal Bureau of Investigation—part of the US government that investigates crime

fingerspelling
way of spelling words with hand movements into a "listener's" hand, sometimes used by deaf people

graduate
someone who has an academic degree

grooved writing board
special board, placed between sheets of paper, with grooves to help blind writers keep their words even

heist
robbery

honorary
given as an honor, or out of respect, and without pay

honors
an award or symbol of excellence or superiority

immigrant
a person who comes to live in a country that he or she was not born in

legislator
someone who makes
and passes laws

lip reading
understanding spoken
words by watching,
or sometimes feeling,
the movement of the
speaker's lips

manual alphabet
different hand positions
to represent each letter
of the alphabet, used
by deaf people to spell

meningitis
serious illness in
which there is swelling
of the brain

Nobel Peace Prize
prize awarded each
year to a person or group
who has worked for
world peace

pacifist
someone who
is against war

plagiarism
using someone else's
words and claiming that
they are your own

poorhouse
building in which poor
people could live in
return for doing work

socialism
belief that a country's
wealth should be shared
equally between its
people, or citizens

sophomore
second-year college
student, or the second
year of college

southern belle
young woman,
usually with a wealthy
background, from the
southern United States

union
organized group of
workers that fights for
better working conditions
and fair pay

vaudeville
type of theater show
popular in the US in
the 1920s

water pump
device that pulls up
water from a well

stage fright
fear felt when talking
or performing in front
of an audience

stroke
serious medical
condition caused by
blockage of a blood
vessel to the brain

suffragist
someone who supports
women's rights

Index

Acknowledgments

DK would like to thank: Jolyon Goddard for additional editorial assistance; Romi Chakraborty and Pallavi Narain for design support; Jacqueline Hornberger for proofreading; Helen Peters for the index; Emily Kimball and Nishani Reed for legal advice; Sue Pilkilton for her expertise on Helen's life; Stephanie Laird for literacy consulting; Audrey Shading for additional consulting; and Noah Harley for serving as our "Kid Editor."

The publisher would like to thank the following for their kind permission to reproduce their photographs:
(Key: a-above; b-below/bottom; c-center; f-far; l-left; r-right; t-top)

7 Depositphotos Inc: Oleksandr_UA (br). 9 Getty Images: SuperStock (cra). 19 Alamy Stock Photo: INTERFOTO. 25 Alamy Stock Photo: The Granger Collection. 26 "Courtesy of Perkins School forthe Blind Archives, Watertown, MA". 28 Dreamstime.com: Georgios Kollidas (clb). 35 Getty Images: DEA / A. DAGLI ORTI. 39 Getty Images: Bettmann. 40 "Courtesy of Perkins School for the Blind Archives, Watertown, MA". 41 Getty Images: Bettmann. 47 Dreamstime.com: Sergey Lavrentev / Laures. 51 "Courtesy of Perkins School for the Blind Archives, Watertown, MA". 52 New England Historic Genealogical Society: Photograph of Helen Keller and Anne Sullivan, Thaxter Parks Spencer Papers, R. Stanton Avery Special Collections, New England Historic Genealogical Society. 54 Alamy Stock Photo: Art Collection 2 (cra). 55 Alamy Stock Photo: Everett Collection Inc. 57 Library of Congress, Washington, D.C.: LC-DIG-ds-05448. 58 Alamy Stock Photo: Granger Historical Picture Archive. 61 Courtesy of the American Foundation for the Blind, Helen Keller Archive. 62 123RF.com: gary718. 66 Alamy Stock Photo: Historic Collection (cra). 69 Alamy Stock Photo: PRILL Mediendesign. 73 Library of Congress, Washington, D.C.: LC-USZ62-78991. 74 Alamy Stock Photo: Historic Collection. 75 Alamy Stock Photo: Pictorial Press Ltd. 76 Library of Congress, Washington, D.C.: LC-USZ62-78762. 82 Schlesinger Library, Radcliffe Institute, Harvard University. 85 Getty Images: Bettmann (cra). Out of the dark : essays, lectures, and addresses on physical and social vision: Helen Keller / Garden City, N.Y. : Doubleday / Brigham Young University / Harold B. Lee Library (clb). 87 Getty Images: Buyenlarge (ca, cb). 88 Getty Images: Hulton Deutsch / Corbis Historical. 93 Getty Images: Bettmann. 95 Getty Images: Hulton Archive / Stringer. 97 CRITICAL PAST LLC: © 2018 CriticalPast LLC (b). Library of Congress, Washington, D.C.: LC-USZ62-32699 (cra). 98 Dreamstime.com: Robwilson39 (cra). 99 "Courtesy of Perkins School for the Blind Archives, Watertown, MA". 101 Alamy Stock Photo: Granger Historical Picture Archive. 103 Courtesy of the American Foundation for the Blind, Helen Keller Archive. 104 "Courtesy of Perkins School for the Blind Archives, Watertown, MA". 105 Dorling Kindersley: Gary Ombler / Royal Airforce Museum, London. 106 Courtesy of the American Foundation for the Blind, Helen Keller Archive: ©Academy of Motion Picture Arts and Sciences® (br). Depositphotos Inc: Oleksandr_UA (tl). 109 Getty Images: Hulton Archive / Stringer. 110 Getty Images: Bettmann (bc)

Cover images: Front and Spine: Alamy Stock Photo: Science History Images

All other images © Dorling Kindersley
For further information see: www.dkimages.com

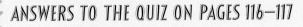

ANSWERS TO THE QUIZ ON PAGES 116–117

1. Ivy Green; 2. Mildred Keller; 3. Anne Sullivan; 4. braille; 5. Sarah Fuller; 6. Radcliffe College; 7. John Macy; 8. *The Story of My Life*; 9. *Deliverance*; 10. American Foundation for the Blind (AFB); 11. a suffragist; 12. Helen Keller International (HKI)